The
Circulatory
System

Where Do I Get My Energy?

Chris Oxlade

raintree

a Capstone company — publishers for children

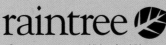

Raintree is an imprint of Capstone Global Library Limited, a company incorporated in England and Wales having its registered office at 7 Pilgrim Street, London, EC4V 6LB – Registered company number: 6695582

www.raintreepublishers.co.uk
myorders@raintreepublishers.co.uk

Edited by Adam Miller, Sian Smith, and Penny West
Designed by Philippa Jenkins
Original illustrations © Capstone Global Library Ltd 2014
Illustrated by Geoff Ward
Picture research by Tracy Cummins
Originated by Capstone Global Library Ltd
Produced by Victoria Fitzgerald
Printed and bound in China by CTPS

ISBN 978 1 406 27431 8 (hardback)
17 16 15 14 13
10 9 8 7 6 5 4 3 2 1

ISBN 978 1 406 27438 7 (paperback)
18 17 16 15 14
10 9 8 7 6 5 4 3 2 1

Oxlade, Chris
The Circulatory System: Where Do I Get My Energy? (Show Me Science)
A full catalogue record for this book is available from the British Library.

Acknowledgements
We would like to thank the following for permission to reproduce photographs:
Alamy p. 19 (© Nucleus Medical Art Inc); Getty Images pp. 4 (David Young-Wolff), 5 (Echo), 17 (Chris Cole), 20 (Stanislaw Pytel), 22 (George Doyle); Photo Researchers pp. 8 (BSIP / Science Source), 10 (Biophoto Associates / Science Source), 11 (Eye of Science / Science Source), 12 (Eye of Science / Science Source), 16 (Alfred Pasieka / Science Source), 18 (Biophoto Associates / Science Source), 23 (Eye of Science / Science Source), 24 (AJ Photo), 27 (Apogee / Science Source); Shutterstock pp. 6 (© Geoffrey Jones), 7 (© Art Allianz), 13 (© Malota), 14 (© Lorelyn Medina), 21 (© sydeen), 26 (© Andrea Danti), 28 (© Vasiliy Koval), Superstock pp.25 (ABK / BSIP), 29 (Blend Images).

Cover photograph reproduced with permission of Getty Images (Jonatan Fernstrom).

We would like to thank Ann Fullick for her invaluable help in the preparation of this book.
Every effort has been made to contact copyright holders of material reproduced in this book. Any omissions will be rectified in subsequent printings if notice is given to the publishers.

Contents

Some words are shown in bold, **like this**. You can find out what they mean by looking in the glossary.

Sugar for energy

It is the day of the big race! You are on the start line, raring to go. On your marks ... get set ... go! You sprint off, with your muscles working hard to make you run fast. Soon your **heart** is thumping in your chest, and you are breathing deeply. The finish line is in sight. You are in second place. You make one last effort, sprint past the leader, and win the race!

HOW MUCH ENERGY?

We count energy in kilocalories (kcal) or kilojoules (kJ). An average adult man needs about 2,500 kcal (10,400 kJ) of energy a day, and an adult woman about 2,000 kcal (8,400 kJ) a day. Children need less energy. People who do action-packed jobs, such as builders and sportspeople, need more energy.

You needed energy to do all that hard work! That energy came from your food. Some of the food was turned into sugar, because your body can get energy from sugar. The sugar moves around your body through your **circulatory system**. This is one of the main systems that makes up your body – it is your body's transport system.

WHAT IS A SUGAR RUSH?

Many children seem to act very excitedly after eating sweets or drinking sugary drinks. Their parents call this a "sugar rush". Eating and drinking does give you energy, but scientists have never found evidence that a "sugar rush" actually exists.

Sugar sources

There are lots of different sugars, with different names. **Glucose** is the sugar that your body uses as a fuel. Energy drinks and sports drinks are full of glucose. Sucrose is another sugar. It is the sugar in granulated sugar and the most common sugar in the food you eat. Other common sugars are fructose and lactose.

Sugary foods

Most natural foods, such as fruits, vegetables, and milk, contain some sugar. Of course, sweet foods, such as sweets, chocolate bars, jam, and honey, contain lots of sugar, because lots of sugar goes into making them. Many other foods, such as cakes and biscuits, have sugar as an ingredient, too. Some foods that you might not think contain sugar, such as breakfast cereals, actually do.

A teaspoon of granulated sugar contains about 20 kcals (85 kJ) of energy. Eating a lot of this kind of sugar is unhealthy.

The nutritional panel on a food packet shows how much sugar the food contains.

Sugar from other substances

Sometimes the particles in sugars are joined up together to make long chains. One of the substances they form is called **starch**. This is the main ingredient in flour, used to make breads, cakes, and biscuits. Starch is also found in vegetables like potatoes and in rice and maize.

In your body, starches are broken up into sugars. Sugars and starches all belong to a family of chemicals called **carbohydrates**. They are the main source of energy for your body. You also get some energy from substances called **fats** and **proteins**, which come from foods such as diary products, meat, and nuts.

The circulatory system

Your **heart** is at the centre of the **circulatory system**, and it pumps **blood** around and around your body, carrying useful materials with it. Two of these materials are sugar and **oxygen**, which your body needs to get energy.

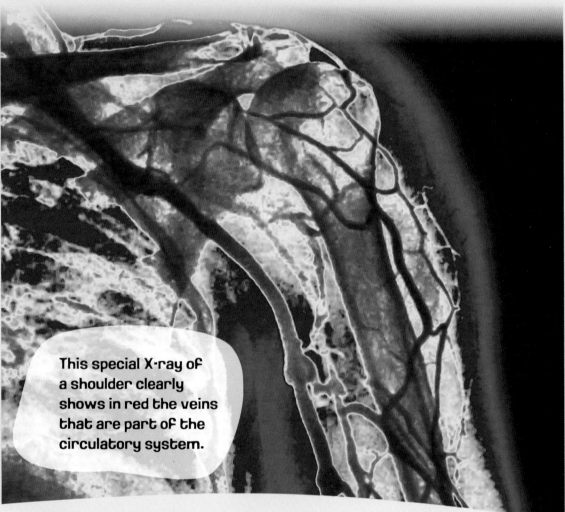

This special X-ray of a shoulder clearly shows in red the veins that are part of the circulatory system.

Harvey and the heart

Until about 400 years ago, most people believed in the theories of a famous Roman doctor called Galen. He thought that blood was one of four liquids in the body – the others being black bile, yellow bile, and phlegm! He also thought that the heart controls whether a person is happy or sad. English doctor William Harvey (1578-1657) was the first person to show that the heart pumps blood.

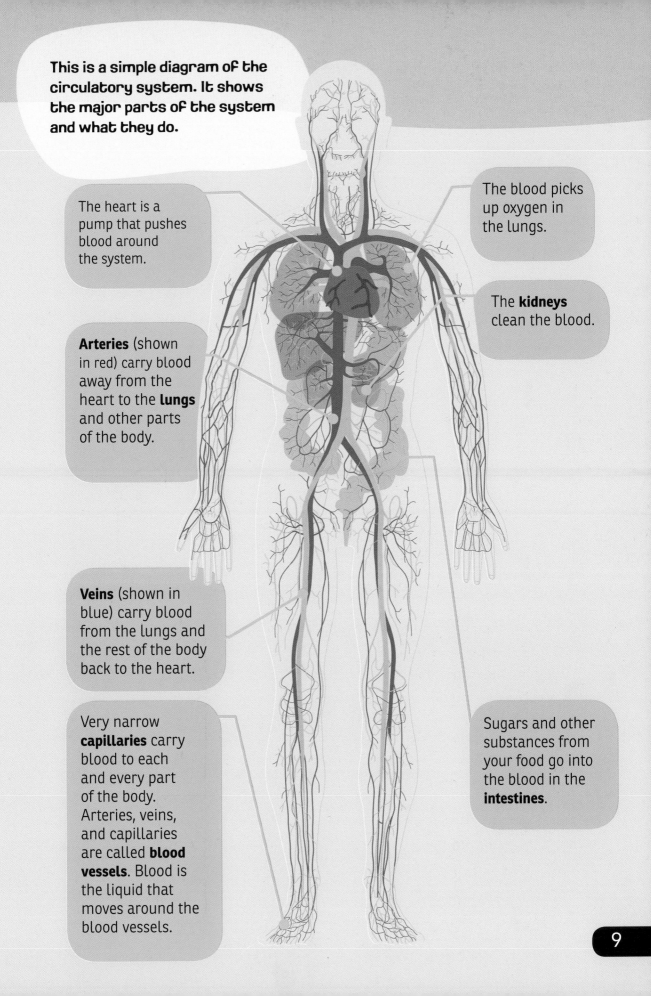

This is a simple diagram of the circulatory system. It shows the major parts of the system and what they do.

The heart is a pump that pushes blood around the system.

The blood picks up oxygen in the lungs.

The **kidneys** clean the blood.

Arteries (shown in red) carry blood away from the heart to the **lungs** and other parts of the body.

Veins (shown in blue) carry blood from the lungs and the rest of the body back to the heart.

Very narrow **capillaries** carry blood to each and every part of the body. Arteries, veins, and capillaries are called **blood vessels**. Blood is the liquid that moves around the blood vessels.

Sugars and other substances from your food go into the blood in the **intestines**.

Sugar starts its journey

Let's see how sugar gets from your food into your **circulatory system**. The journey starts when you put food into your mouth. Your mouth is at the start of your body's **digestive system**. The digestive system breaks up food into tiny particles, ready to go into your **blood**.

Chewing and swallowing

Chewing food is the first step in **digestion**. Chewing breaks food into smaller chunks before you swallow it. Your mouth also makes saliva. This contains chemicals that begin to break up any **carbohydrates** in the food into sugars.

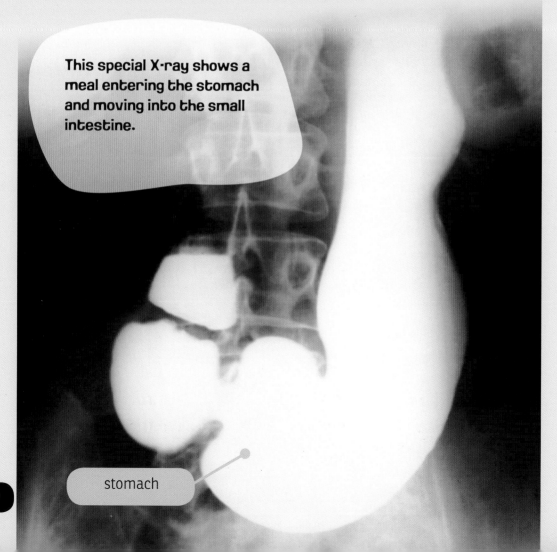

This special X-ray shows a meal entering the stomach and moving into the small intestine.

stomach

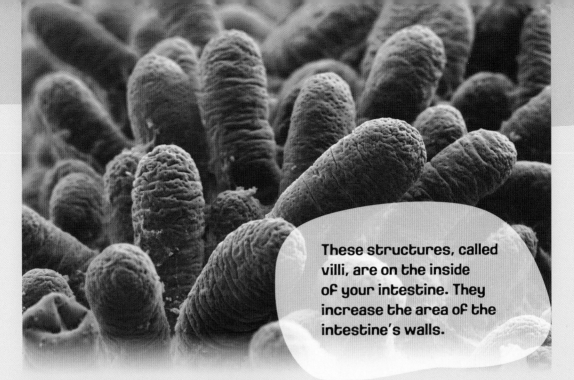

These structures, called villi, are on the inside of your intestine. They increase the area of the intestine's walls.

The digestive system

When you swallow, the food moves down into your stomach. Your stomach is a bag made of muscle. It churns the food and starts to break down the **proteins**. Then the food goes on into the small **intestine**. Here more chemicals get to work, breaking down the carbohydrates into different sugars. After a few hours, most carbohydrates have been broken down into **glucose**. Proteins and **fats** are broken down, too.

Into the blood

Millions of **capillaries** are in the intestine walls. Glucose moves into the blood flowing through these capillaries.

Strong acids

There are very powerful acids in your stomach that kill any harmful **bacteria** in your food. The acids are so strong they could strip paint from wood! Your stomach is protected from these acids by special mucus. This stops the stomach from digesting itself!

Blood bits

An adult has about 5 litres (about 10 pints) of **blood**. About half of this blood is made up of a yellowy liquid called **plasma**, which is mostly water. **Glucose** and other sugars are dissolved in the plasma. You cannot see them because their particles are so tiny. It is just the same as when you stir sugar into a drink – the sugar seems to disappear because it breaks up, but it is still there. Other substances being transported around the body, such as **minerals**, **proteins**, and **hormones**, are also dissolved in the plasma.

These are red blood cells (and white blood cells), magnified about 5,000 times.

Giving blood

People injured in accidents or having operations sometimes lose lots of blood. They are given blood that people have donated. There are different types of blood. If the patient is given the wrong type of blood, the red **cells** clump together and clog up the **capillaries**. Before doctors understood this, people often died after they were given blood! Now donated blood saves thousands of lives every year.

A blood type called O negative is very important. It never causes clumping, so it can be given to any patient.

Blood cells

The rest of your blood is made up of blood cells – red ones and white ones. Red blood cells give blood its red colour. They transport **oxygen** from the **lungs** to the rest of your body (there is more about this on page 18). White blood cells help to fight diseases and infections in your body (there is more about this on page 23).

Your body's pump

Now that sugars are in your **blood**, they need to get to where they are needed. That means the blood has to move around the **circulatory system**, carrying the sugars with it. The blood does not flow on its own. It needs to be pumped, and that is the job of your **heart**.

Muscle that never tires

Most muscles in your body get tired if they keep working, but your heart muscle never gets tired. On average, a heart beats about 70 times a minute. That is about 4,200 times an hour, about 100,000 times a day, and over 36 million times a year!

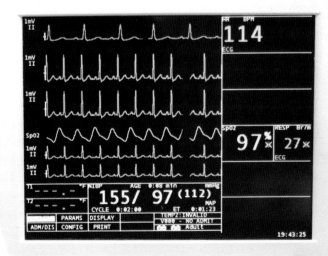

This machine is a cardiac monitor. It shows each beat of a patient's heart muscles and the heart rate.

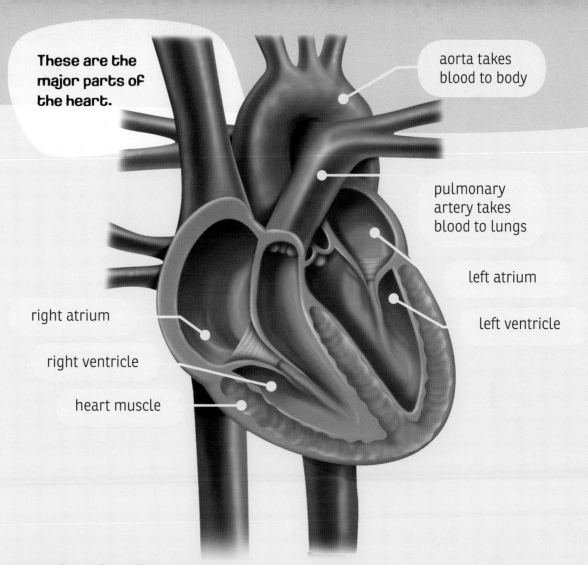

These are the major parts of the heart.

aorta takes blood to body

pulmonary artery takes blood to lungs

left atrium

left ventricle

right atrium

right ventricle

heart muscle

Inside the heart

The heart is about the size of a clenched fist, and it is made of muscle. Inside there are four spaces called chambers, which are full of blood. Every second or so, the muscles contract (get shorter). This is a heartbeat. The beat makes the chambers smaller, which pushes the blood out of the heart and into the **arteries**. Valves in the heart make sure the blood only flows one way out of the heart.

The heart has two sides. One side pumps blood to the **lungs**, where it collects **oxygen** (see page 18). The blood then returns to the other side of the heart and is pumped to the other parts of the body. Then it returns to the heart and is pumped to the lungs again.

Sugar to the cells

The **blood** that comes from **capillaries** around your stomach and **intestines** is full of chemicals from **digested** food. These include **glucose** (the sugar your body gets energy from) and chemicals from **fats** and **proteins**. The blood flows along **veins** to an **organ** called the liver – your body's chemical factory. One of its jobs is to break up some chemicals from fats and proteins to make more glucose.

Glucose and respiration

You can think of glucose as a fuel for the **cells**. It moves from your blood into your cells. In the cells, a series of chemical reactions take place. These turn the energy in the glucose into a form the cells can use. This process is called respiration. Respiration also needs **oxygen** to happen (see page 18).

This microscope image shows a network of capillaries taking blood to cells.

Exercise uses up glucose in the blood.

Storing energy

Soon after you eat a meal, glucose starts going into your blood. Often your body does not need all the glucose right away. So the liver turns some of the leftover glucose into a material called glycogen. This is stored in your liver or in your muscles. The glycogen is turned back into the glucose when it is needed.

You can only store a certain amount of glycogen. If there is too much of it, it gets turned into fat, which is also stored in your body. The fat can be turned back into glucose later, but if you store too much fat, it can be bad for your health.

Vital oxygen

Your **cells** need **oxygen** as well as **glucose** for respiration to happen. The oxygen comes from the air around you. It gets to your cells through your **lungs** and then goes through your **circulatory system**.

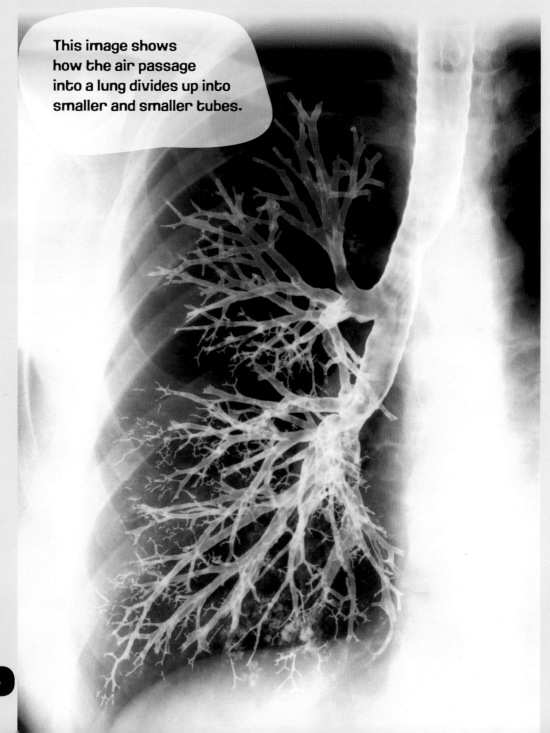

This image shows how the air passage into a lung divides up into smaller and smaller tubes.

Red blood cell facts

Red blood cells are very small. A tiny drop contains millions of them, and a thimbleful contains about ten billion of them! The cells live to do their job for about three months, then die. The materials in them are recycled to make new red blood cells. The new ones are made in your bone marrow – about two million of them every second!

Blood visits your lungs as it moves around the circulatory system. It passes along **capillaries** close to the inside surfaces of your lungs. When you breathe in, air containing oxygen goes into your lungs. Some of the oxygen passes into your blood. The blood returns to your **heart** and is then pumped around your body. When the blood arrives at cells, the oxygen moves into the cells.

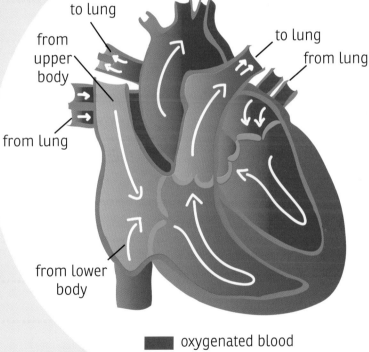

This picture shows how blood moves through the heart.

to lung

from upper body

from lung

to lung

from lung

from lung

from lower body

■ oxygenated blood
■ deoxygenated blood

Red blood cells

Oxygen is carried by red blood cells. Inside the cells is a chemical called haemoglobin. This traps the oxygen when the blood visits the lungs and releases it again when the blood visits cells. After the blood visits the lungs and is carrying oxygen, it is bright red. After it gives up its oxygen to cells, it goes a dark, red-blue colour.

Getting rid of waste

Imagine a log burning in a campfire. Slowly the wood burns away until there is almost nothing left. The chemicals in the wood have reacted with **oxygen** in the air, and the reaction has made water (given off in smoke) and a gas called **carbon dioxide**. Respiration, which happens in the **cells** in your body, is the same sort of reaction as burning. **Glucose** reacts with oxygen, and carbon dioxide and water are formed. You need to get rid of the carbon dioxide because it is poisonous!

On a cold morning, you can see water vapour coming out of your mouth. There is carbon dioxide with the water vapour.

Letting out blood

Until about 150 years ago, doctors thought that some illnesses, such as fevers and headaches, were caused by patients having too much **blood**. Their treatment was to make a cut and let some blood out! This was called bloodletting. Leeches were sometimes put on a patient's skin to suck the blood out instead.

Today, doctors sometimes use leeches to help repair skin. The leeches help blood flow around wounds.

Waste into the blood

Water and carbon dioxide move out of your cells and into the blood in **capillaries** that pass close by. Blood from the capillaries flows into the **veins**, which carry the blood back to the **heart**. From there the blood is pumped to the **lungs**. Here, the carbon dioxide passes out of the blood and into the air inside the lungs. When you breathe out, the carbon dioxide passes out of your body.

More jobs for your circulatory system

So far, we have seen that your **circulatory system** transports **glucose** from the **digestive system** to **cells** to give the cells energy. It also transports **oxygen** from **lungs** to cells, where it is needed for respiration. It carries waste, such as **carbon dioxide**, away from cells. But there are other jobs that the circulatory system does.

When you cut yourself, blood helps to fix the wound.

White blood cells

White **blood** cells are always on the warpath in your body. Their mission is to seek out and destroy germs (**bacteria** and **viruses**). They creep along **blood vessels** by changing shape again and again, and can even squeeze through blood vessel walls. When a white cell finds a germ, it wraps itself around the germ and **digests** it.

Here, white blood cells are engulfing bacteria (the orange bits), magnified about 2,000 times.

Carrying messages

The blood carries chemical messengers called **hormones** around the body. The hormones are released in one part of the body and control how other parts of the body work. One example is the hormone adrenaline. When you are scared, your body releases adrenaline into the blood. When adrenaline reaches the **heart**, it makes the heart beat faster. This gets your body ready to fight or run away.

Mending damage

Blood contains many tiny particles called platelets. When you cut yourself, platelets gather at the site of the damage. They react with other chemicals in the blood. This makes a sticky web that blocks up the wound and makes the blood clot.

Controlling blood sugar

The amount of **glucose** in the **blood** is called your blood sugar level. If your blood sugar level gets too high or too low, you feel very ill. A **hormone** called **insulin**, which is made in the pancreas, controls your blood sugar level for you.

Diabetic people inject themselves with insulin when necessary.

Insulin at work

When your blood sugar level rises, insulin is released. When the insulin reaches your **cells**, it makes them take in glucose from the blood. It also makes the liver store any excess glucose as glycogen. Then when glucose levels in the blood start to fall, the insulin level drops again, so not too much glucose is taken out of the blood.

Losing control

People who suffer from **diabetes** cannot control their level of blood sugar. This is because they cannot make enough insulin, or their insulin does not work properly. Glucose can build up in their blood, which can damage the body's cells. People who suffer from diabetes control their condition by taking injections of insulin, eating a healthy diet, and exercising.

Falling too far

If a diabetic person injects too much insulin, does not eat properly, or does too much exercise, their blood sugar level can fall too far. This is called hypoglycemia. A diabetic person who starts shaking and sweating, goes pale, and has a high pulse may be experiencing hypoglycaemia. They need to take some sugar straight away.

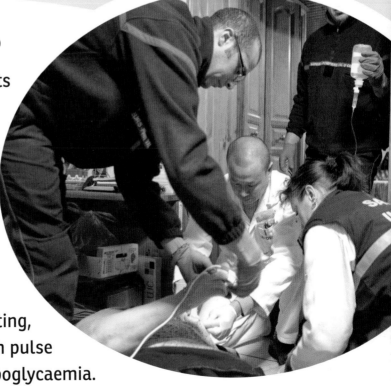

Fault finding

The **circulatory system** is an amazing system that works all day, every day, carrying out all its jobs for you. But sometimes things can go wrong.

Blocked blood vessels

People who eat too much sugary food are likely to get **fatty** material sticking to the insides of their **arteries**. The fatty lumps make the arteries narrow, so less **blood** can flow through them. In the arteries that supply blood to the **heart**, this is called coronary heart disease.

Sometimes blood clots around these fatty lumps. The clot can block the artery where it forms, or can break away and block an artery somewhere else. The **cells** in that part of the body cannot work properly without their supply of **oxygen**. If this part is the brain, a person can have a stroke, where part of the brain begins to die. If it is the heart, the person can have a heart attack. The heart stops pumping blood properly because the heart muscles cannot work. Strokes and heart attacks can be fatal.

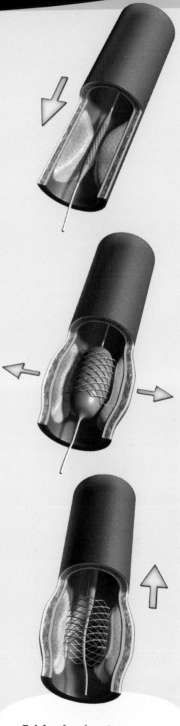

A blocked artery can be opened up with a stent – a tiny balloon surrounded by a fine wire mesh.

Tiny heart surgery

With high-tech medical scanners, doctors can detect heart problems in babies as the babies are growing inside their mothers. These problems include holes between the heart's chambers and arteries that join to the heart in the wrong place. Incredibly, surgeons can fix a baby's heart before it is born, even though the heart can be as small as a grape!

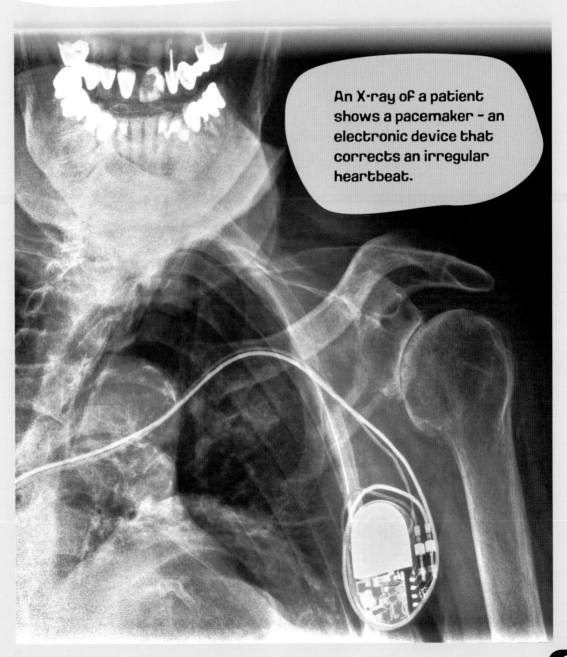

An X-ray of a patient shows a pacemaker – an electronic device that corrects an irregular heartbeat.

Sugar in the balance

In this book, we have seen that sugar is not just a sweet-tasting substance found in sweets and drinks. It is the source of energy for all the **cells** in your body, and it is transported around by your **circulatory system**.

> This balanced meal contains a mixture of substances your body needs.

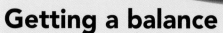

Getting a balance

You do not have to eat lots of sugar to get energy. Your body makes **glucose** from **carbohydrates**, **fats**, and **proteins**, too. So you should eat a good mixture of bread and pasta, fruit and vegetables, fish and meat, grains, nuts, and dairy foods. This is known as a balanced diet. It contains a good mixture of the substances your body needs, including proteins, fats, vitamins, and **minerals**, as well as carbohydrates for energy.

An occasional sugary treat does no harm!

Good and bad energy sources

Eating too much sugar causes problems. If your body cannot use all the sugar, it gets stored as fats in your body. This can lead to people becoming overweight and can also lead to **heart** disease. Of course, eating sugary food can also rot your teeth.

You should get about half your energy from carbohydrates (and only a little of that from sugars), and the rest from fats and proteins. Normally it is best to get energy from foods such as wholegrain bread, beans, and lentils. These are **digested** and broken down into glucose slowly, and so release their energy slowly. Eating sugary things gives you an energy boost, but this can run out quickly.

Glossary

artery blood vessel that carries blood away from the heart and to the different parts of the body

bacteria tiny, single-celled living thing

blood fluid that flows around the circulatory system, made up mainly of plasma and blood cells

blood vessel tube that carries blood around the body

capillary tiny blood vessel that takes blood to the individual cells in the body

carbohydrate substance that is a source of energy in food

carbon dioxide often a waste gas in a body process, also found in the air

cell tiny unit that all living things are made out of

circulatory system system in the body that moves materials around the body in the blood

diabetes disease that means a person cannot properly control the level of glucose in the blood

digestion process of breaking down food into small chemicals that are useful to the body

digestive system system in the body that takes useful substances, such as sugars, fats, and proteins, out of food

fat substance that is the main ingredient in animal and vegetable fats

glucose type of sugar that is the source of energy for cells in the body

heart organ that pumps blood around the circulatory system

hormone chemical messenger that moves through the circulatory system and controls parts of the body

insulin hormone that controls the level of glucose in the blood

intestine long tube that is part of the digestive system, where food is broken up into simpler substances that move into the blood

kidney organ that helps to clean the blood and removes excess water from the blood

lung organ in the body where oxygen moves into the blood, and carbon dioxide moves out of the blood

mineral natural substance in food that your body needs to work properly

organ body part that does a specific job

oxygen gas that is part of the air, needed by all plants and animals

plasma yellowy, liquid part of the blood

protein material that is the building block for making the parts of living things, such as muscles and nerves

starch carbohydrate found in foods, such as potatoes, bread, and pasta

vein blood vessel that carries blood from different parts of the body back to the heart

virus tiny piece of material that can cause diseases if it gets into your body, such as a cold virus

Find out more

Books

Blood, Bones and Body Bits (Horrible Science), Nick Arnold and Tony De Saulles (Scholastic, 2008)

Heart and Blood (Body Focus), Carol Ballard (Heinemann Library, 2009)

What is My Pulse? (Inside My Body), Carol Ballard (Raintree, 2012)

Websites

kidshealth.org/kid/diabetes_basics/what/type1.html
You will find information about diabetes on this website.

kidshealth.org/kid/htbw
Here you will find interactive information about how the body, including the heart and circulatory system, works.

www.medbio.info/horn/sugars4kids
This website has lots of information about sugar and how your body digests it.

www.smm.org/heart
You can look at interactive information about the heart and lungs from the Science Museum of Minnesota.

Places to visit

Thackray Medical Museum
Beckett Street
Leeds
LS9 7LN
www.thackraymuseum.org

The Science Museum
Exhibition Road
South Kensington
London
SW7 2DD
www.sciencemuseum.org.uk

Index